Sweet and Sour

For

The Free Spirit

Poems by Elizabeth Terzian

Illustrations by Hera Terzian

iUniverse, Inc.

New York   Bloomington

Sweet and Sour for the Free Spirit

iUniverse books may be ordered through booksellers or by contacting:

iUniverse
1663 Liberty Drive
Bloomington, IN 47403
www.iuniverse.com
1-800-Authors (1-800-288-4677)

ISBN: 978-1-4401-2273-6 (pbk)
ISBN: 978-1-4401-2274-3 (ebk)

Library of Congress Control Number: 2009922574

Printed in the United States of America

iUniverse rev. date: 5/22/2009

Dedicated in loving memory to Maria Doubrovsky
teacher, friend, and kindred free spirit

Author's Note

My intention is to honor our humanity and be able to laugh at our shortcomings. In this regard, I have been influenced by the spirit of the French eighteenth-century authors La Bruyère, La Fontaine, and Voltaire. An offended feeling should arise in the reader it is the ego's identification with the shadow. The intensity of the feeling will then determine the measure of identification. Names, characters, places, and incidents used are purely fictitious. Any resemblance to real people, organizations, or institutions is unintentional.

Acknowledgments

I am grateful to The Circle of Muses for their generous responses to the poems: Edie Barrett, Cheryl De Ciantis, Leanna Falcon, Sherri Mendenhall, and Laura Seitz. Your amused reaction to my readings prompted me to publish these poems. For the digital graphics, I am grateful to Raffi Shubukian. Your mastery of computers and images is outstanding.

Finally, all thanks to my husband and children who not only offered their support but were also my first audience: Berj for your love and encouragement; Raffi for your patience and assistance with computer technicality; and last but not least Hera for the empathy and artistic spirit you bring in your illustrations.

Contents

The Little Green Gnome

A gentle cracking sound I heard
From the heart of an oak
Whose there? I asked, surprised
A little green gnome
Hiding behind an acorn replied
"It is I who dwell in the roots
Of this mighty oak
To heal
To protect the forest trees and folks
And keep their zest and rest unstirred
I work in silence, underground
For my love of the earth is profound."
So, the centuries' old little gnome
Embalmed my petrified soul
And vanished swiftly in a tree hole

The Wildflower

Nobody knows how many there are
Lost in a civilized desert
Graveyard of souls
Drowned in a swamp
Where slugs and mites
    Thrive
    In the midst
Of smug fungi and humbugs.
There, surrounded by weeds
Between the shepherd's purse
And the Venus' flytrap
Pure, beautiful, unique
A wildflower I found
Waiting to be revived
Quick
Before the blight

The Linden Tree

There was a flood
        In the Lord's backyard
A linden tree cried and cried
Fauna and Flora gathered around
It was a mystery so profound
"What's the matter?"
        They all together inquired
"I need to be loved,"
        She modestly replied
Her beauty and grief
        Touched the Lord
He loved her such
That her tears
Changed into heart-shaped leaves

Birches Don't Need Pruning

Birches don't need pruning
The title of a book perhaps?
But no!
The heart wrenching truth
Every birch would tell you
If you listen carefully
Keeping an ear close to the trunk
Lips kissing the bark soft and white
Hands caressing the leaves.
Many had fallen victim
Under the axe
Of a gardener unseasoned and green.
Amputated of their limbs
They sing the sorrow of their loss.
Birches are born to inspire beauty
Let the Creator be in charge
How ever noble your intention may be

The Dormant Grove

The muses caught
In cobwebbed trees
Pearls of dew
On frozen strings
Crystal stars
In opaque sound
Death lurks all around
The dryads cry
Nobody hears
Only the gods of nature
Know

The Cry of the Tree

Trees cry when they're cut
Agonizing in the middle of the night
The timberman finished her off
He drew her sap
Crushed the leaves
Skinned the bark
Cut branches and twigs
The trunk got hollow
The roots got dry
Young in years
Old in pain
Droplets of blood
Dripped of her breasts
Her womb was sacked
Her guts removed
Dismembered
The tree fell dead
Her cries
Fell on deaf ears

The Twin Sister of Death

This old tree
Whose roots are drenched
Can no longer hold sap in its veins
Dried and brittle
The vessel is empty
The tomb is cold
She calls upon fire
To consume her to ashes
Time has come
To meet face to face
The mysterious stranger
Whom she nurtured inside her flesh
"I thought your name was Love," she said
"But you're no other than
The twin sister of death"

Elegy for a Son

I am the hollow tree

Through which the wind sings

The universal plaintive song

Of suffering souls

Of wombs torn to bits

By grief

Sudden and violent

Wild dogs biting

At her belly

At her tender flesh sore

The Caterpillar

Through the hole of a leaf
             I munched
I saw the beak of a bird
             I feared
Quickly I crawled
             And hid
From the merciless pries
Of a predator's eyes

Still and brave
I held my breath
Waiting for fate
             To decide
Which of the two
Meal or butterfly
I am destined
             To comply

Woman

The praying mantis had two offsprings
Who used to live just like kings
She didn't care as such herself
Humble at heart
Of the world's goods
She craved much less
A mate she kept
To provide
Who longed for her
Neck and legs
For extra favors
She killed him first
And surely
Mated next
Evil
She's labeled for
A survival instinct
Nature's gift

Lady Walrus

Lady Walrus
Queen of her household
Couldn't keep a necklace
On her bull-necked throat
For she was busy
Swallowing
Creatures of the sea
Wallowing
Heavy, fat, and discontent
Lady Walrus
Couldn't understand
Why her square-jawed neck
Wasn't regal kept

Dr. Mole Psychiatrist

Dr. Mole had poor eyesight
And ventured to cure
His fellow neighbors.
He claimed sunlight
To be the culprit
The height of trees
The cause of ailment
The flight in the open air
A sure danger.
He labored, operated
And diligently led his patients
To his close fitting quarters
Where they'll recover
And restore their health
To tunnel vision, he thought.
The creatures yelled, screamed
And pleaded to be heard
But no sorrow could travel across
Those burrows
No word could penetrate
Someone with no visible ears at all
But with a snout
No doubt
In search of delectable
Gullible food
Aliment for his stomach
Condiment for his ego

Peacock

The peacock entered the palace
Crowded with small animals and fowl
Shading his crested head
He zigzagged down the hall
Fanning his blue green plumage
Shimmering under gold
But no one seemed to notice
The pavonine display of beauty
Since all eyes were level
With his poor modest feet
Dangling from the Louis XV settee
On which he sat waiting
Hopelessly
For flattery

The Bat

Angry
She hits her wings frantically
Against the walls of her cell
Breaking the nocturnal silence
In syncopated flips
Scared
She withdraws at dawn
To the left upper corner of her pallet
And cries
Cries for acceptance
For Unconditional love
For help

The Legend of the Swan

One magical day
In serendipitous times
When the gods and goddesses
Held a banquet on beautiful earth
The naiads hosted a feast to celebrate
The birth of a swan.
All the birds of the sky
And the fish of rivers and seas
Were invited.
The graces bestowed on her the gifts of beauty
The muses offered the talents of letters and arts
They placed her in the care of
Learned women and men
Who, spellbound
Grew fond of her beauty
And admired her wisdom and grace.
Our hosts decided to keep her
For rare and precious was such an adornment
To the glory of their manor.
Considered part of the scenery
With passing times, she was forsaken completely.
Day after day, doleful and elegant
A white plumage
Continued to glide peacefully
On the calm waters of the lake
Until one mysterious hour
The bright-haired Dysis
Presided over her flight
Our limnetic creature
No longer swam
But stretched her wings
And flew away
To new shores
Where her beauty and light
Could forever shine

The Exotic Bird

A little bird
With rainbow plumes
And a song
In his heart
To charm princes and dukes
Enraptured by his spell
The town people
Caught him in a cage
Made of gold
And showed him around
For all to applaud
"Now sing for us," they insisted
But the bird stayed mute
He could only sing
When his heart was content
Prestige, honor and glory
He never wished for
Men's ambitions
Were not his own
He was born free
An exotic bird was he

Puppy Louis at Your Service

"Darling, fetch my slippers,"
Said Madam.
Puppy Louis obeyed instantly.
He was an ingenious dog
Who could cook, write, paint
Drive a car
And even give healing massages
To his mistress and her company.
He wore many hats
During the day
Played the escort in society
During most evenings
And tended on Madam on four paws.
Louis was the dream
Of any middle aged woman
Who chose to live alone
But … nevertheless
A companion enjoyed indeed
Who served her unconditionally.
Our puppy felt so fortunate
Or so he thought
To be loved in return
By a woman aristocratic he found
Classy, charming, and erudite.
Poor little puppy, so naïve
At night, alone on his bed
He stared at the stars
And dreamed quite big
Of liberating humanity
From dysfunctional relationships
When his own leash
Wouldn't allow him
To go further than
His meager sack of kibbles
And his cracked porcelain bowl of water

The Three Rats

Three hungry rats
Went one day
To their neighbor the bird
Asking for some food.

She offered her crop
They gobbled so fast
And craved for more
Wanting all in store.

Soon there was no more.
So they turned to their hostess
Plucked her feathers
Flayed her skin
Jagged her flesh
Six pairs of metal sharp teeth
Sheared her bones
Cut her heart to pieces.

A generous feast indeed
Where nothing was spared
All disappeared.
Our voracious fiends
Swiftly vanished
Searching for a new friend to kill
Only a red spotted leaf remained
Witness
To their lethal deed

Social Rats

The sewage rat
Has seen the light
Shining mud
Gold in his sight
Drooling his tongue
Hung in wonder
He swam to new shores
He liked to explore
He called his friends
For this place was heaven
And soon the river
Became the sewer

More of Social Rats

A magician rat
Who ran out of scarves,
Pigeons, rabbits, and stars
Emptied all drawers and hats
Changed his color
Changed his smile
His crotoline tongue
Ran out of food
And vespine poison
Couldn't find a new brood
A trusting friend he saw
With a cryptic smile he called
To the eternal place
Where he dwells
When the friend refused
To join him there
The coprophilous rat
Spat dung everywhere

The Buffaloes

A herd of buffaloes I once met
Strange as I thought
I mingled through.
They headed one way
Traveled in dusty clouds
Calling it skies
For that met their eyes
Is it poor eyesight or self-righteousness
Inborn or acquired
I don't know
Once revered by ancient tribes
Arrogance
They carry in their souls and minds
Vestige of their noble rights
To judge, to condemn, to accuse
To criticize and to abuse
But who would really want to stay
With such a species and be prey
One's food
Another's rood
You can't change them
You can't tame them
Unless you join their company
You have no choice but to flee
And find a breed with whom you agree
If you want to stay unsmeared
Of the hypocrisy
Of the bourgeoisie, our modern Pharisees
For they don't hear, see, nor feel
All they know is to jeer
Trampling human lives along
Buffaloes, in every corner I meet

Predator

Carrion eater
With piercing eyes
Your name hides
The venom in disguise
Cotton mouth
You rejoice in catching
Your prey dead or alive
You like to seize, tease
Torture and tear
Your victim's flesh
To bits apart
Is this the law of nature
Or man and civilization alike?

Miss Weathervane, Ballet Mistress

The old theatre's weathervane
Grew weary of the four winds
A ballet mistress
She longed to be
Therefore she whirled her way
To the dance floor and stage
Pirouettes were favorite moves
Toward wealthy pupils
Her efforts were used
Perfection she claimed
And held the keys
To the dead masters' ways
Vain you may say
Our ballet mistress is
Despite her monetary gain
And fame
A weathervane
She nevertheless remains

The Sculptor and the Rock

An invincible rock
In the kingdom of men
Scared away all specimen

A jolly old sculptor
Running out of clay
Stopped on his way
By this sight to wonder

He brought his hammer
Saw and pitcher
Point, claw, grit, and chisel

He bruised the stone
Brushed off the dust
Smoothed the angles
Cut, carved the corners

He stuck and drilled
Day and night
Until he reached
Its core in shock

A pretty hollyhock
He found in there
Inspiring vigor
To living debonair

Graveyards of Knowledge

A school I visited
Thought inhabited
For memorial plates
Were engraved
On every classroom door
Of concrete massive shapes.
The insides were rich
With decorated walls
I wasn't sure
Whether I was in Pharaoh's vaults
Only epitaphs were missing.
Schools,
Mausolea of learning
Where the mind shrinks
And the heart wrings

Mausoleum
OF
Learning

Los Angeles, 1995

In this time and place
Trends of all sorts
Happen to be in grace
Such as a hippo in shorts
Roaming all over town
A glorified display
Of jumbo fleshy thighs
For others a sport car
Pierced nostrils, lips, and eyebrows
For traditional tastes
Splendid homes, sculpted nails
For high spirits and intellects
Names, degrees, and clout
Aren't we all proud
To follow the crowd
For all we have
Is all we are
And once we drain
All we have gained
All we are
Seems so bizarre

The Old Pot's Legacy

The big family pot
Had a huge crack
The crack got wide
The crack got deep
No one saw
No one indeed

At sunrise and sunset
Three generations huddled around
The dining room table sound

Until one day
The pot blew up
Letting the soup spill hot

They all went to bed that night
With no dinner
But an insight

Care we give
And care we receive
Are an inseparable pair
For us to be aware

Angels of Death

There is nothing divine
About angels who sit
On marble stones
To lead the souls to heaven
To protect their earthy rotten flesh
They run a chill through my spine
Where the cypress grows dull and tall
Their icy cold features frighten me
"Father, I'm hungry,
        Feed my soul,"
Cries a child nearby
"I am lost among the tombstones
        Searching for you"
There goes a living angel
Whose tears give me warmth

The Upright Dead

"I have a shadow just like you,"
Said the telephone post to the tree standing by.
"The little girl in the house across
Calls her mother to comfort her at night.
Children see crawling shadows
Through open windows
And with great emotion
Express their fears and sorrows
But you my friend
Who walk in the darkness of daylight
You've grown accustomed to your surrounding
Dead is your reaction
Stark is your gaze
A shroud covers your eyes
An invisible coffin limits your space"

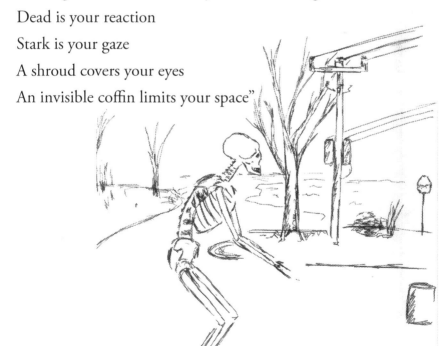

The Crippled Heart

A gut-wrenching world
I ventured to
The day I decided
To be born to
Half-way through
My journey
Lonely, hungry and thirsty
I remained on a rocky road
Half-blind
With dust thrown into my eyes
Deafened by lies
Abandoned with a crippled heart
I cried
I prayed
And the answer to my plea came
"Better a crippled heart than none"

A Woman's Heart

The earth is cold

Biting frost

Choking dusty taste

Gray pain

The damp smell of wet ashes

Crystal salt of tears

Have eaten up her heart

An empty shell of skin

Pumped out of its blood

Dried out of its flesh

Giving

Giving endlessly

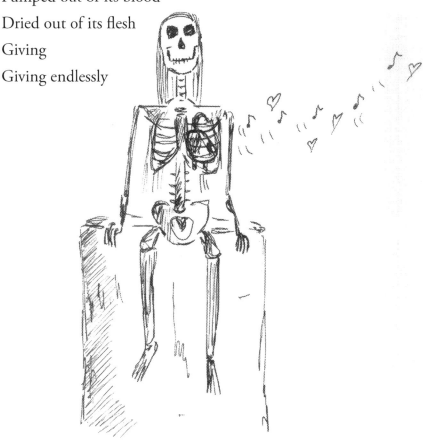

A Heart in Blue

A heart in blue
Asked one day:
"Death, silence, rest
When is it time
For me to resurrect?"
And the answer came
From Death itself:
"Time and Space are human made
To organize and comprehend
For God
Who always likes to play
Such things have no way"

A Love Prescription

Have you ever held a rose to your cheek?
Go to your garden
Choose a rose
Close your eyes
And bring her near
Feel her delicate moist petals
Blending with the musk of your skin
Breathe her into your heart
And give her a smile
For that's all she needs

Don Quixote in Jeans and Sneakers

Have I seen you sweep
      The old man's porch?

Have I seen you carry
      A cripple across the river?

Have I seen you feed
      A child hungry and poor?

Have I seen you console
      The heart of a wretched prisoner?

Have I seen you rescue
      An innocent soul?

Have I seen you befriend a holy fool?

Jean Valjean would have done it
Andrei Karamazov would have been there
But you, dear friend
Aren't you rather
Staring endlessly at the windmills
Building castles in Spain
You dream big
      Act little
Think brave
      Behave coward
Tell tall tales of universal proportions
Are you not the harsh critic of humanity
      Distorting reality
      To fit your theory?

Ruthless Compassion

What is worse than being guided
  By a blind teacher?

What is worse than being ruled
  By a monarch who believes he is enlightened?

What is worse than being called a Christian Fundamentalist
  By an Astrology Fundamentalist?

What is worse than being accused of practicing a religion devotedly
  By a zealot of psychology, astrology, and tarot reading?

What is worse than being enslaved and used
  By someone in the name of friendship and love?

What is worse than trusting oneself
  To someone who dreams of liberating others
  When he himself is drowned in his own emotional vomit?

What is worse than crossing personal boundaries
  And calling it intimacy?

What is worse than accepting
  To live someone else's fantasy?

What is worse than violating someone's feelings,
  Dishonoring the divine mystery of their being
  And hiding behind the mask of good intentions?

What is worse than offering a person
  An opportunity for addiction to an altered state of consciousness
  Insisting and persisting against that person's will?

What is worse than not comprehending
   That another being may have a different lifestyle than one's own
   And be completely fulfilled and happy?

What is worse than a new aficionado to spirituality
   Who wants to initiate a zaddik?

What is worse than accusing someone of distorted imagination
   For expressing feelings and insights into relationships?

What is worse than claiming the practice of ruthless compassion
   And rejecting it vehemently when offered in return?

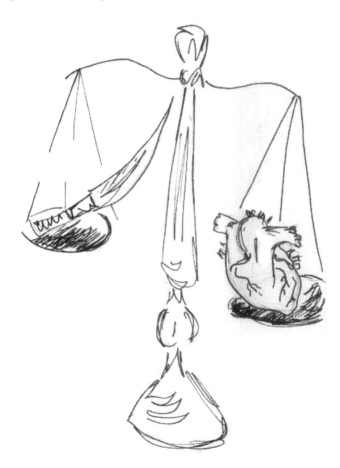

Identity

Eyes of feather
Eyes of gold
Shimmering stars
In a dark gloomy night
A white daisy
Among elegant weed
Turning her face
Toward the sun
To breathe
"It is I,"
Said she
To her Creator
"Just the way
You want me to be"

Confused

I have reached
>> For a flower
>>>> And was pricked by a thorn

I have smiled
>> At the sunshine
>>>> And was scorched to the bone

I have picked
>> A little bunny
>>>> And was crushed with a stone

I fed a deer
>> And was spat on the face
>>>> By a toad

I have met many hardships
>> In this life as a soul

>> Still, I don't understand

39

Humility

On a cold winter night
A beggar knocked at a door
"I have not much to offer,"
Said a man on the porch
And handed her a bowl of vinegar
"Thank you," replied the beggar
"You're most generous
For I'll sharpen my sense of smell
Bathe
And ground myself with"

Disenchantment

A deflated heart
Flatly bored
Lives on a plane
Different from all
Cigarette burn holes
On a blistered membrane
God within killed
Enthusiasm flown

Existential Bargain

A bum's heart
A lady's shell
A ticket to heaven
Twenty dollars I read
Should I bargain
Should I accept
Perhaps it's cheaper
Than being in hell
House, car, luxury
Clothes and friends
Bank accounts, clout
Expenses and stress
Paid in time and energy
Body, soul, integrity

Rejection

Rejection is a knife

Cutting across a vulnerable belly

A dagger thrust between

Two innocent breasts

Rejection is a bitter venom

It seeps through the pores

     Of your skin

Into each cell of your body

Into the depth of your soul

Rejection is the annihilation of your being

     By the other

The Rejected Gift

Act or react

In a perfect world

Where words fall

On hard rock

Like rain on wasteland

Words that drip

From the heart's

Deepest wound

An opening of the veil

Through which

The divine light

Reveals the truth of a soul

In pain

"Be alert, friend

Open your eyes and ears

Heed the Spirit

For the gift

It brings"

The Shadow of Rejection

Befriend rejection

Trust in its ways

A compass that indicates

All the places to be

Except the one you know

Where not to be

Protection it brings

From a road not meant to travel by

From people better off without

Celebrate rejection

Everyday you breathe

For it helps you

See, accept, and understand

The uniqueness of your person and life

Rejection is an affirmation of being

A gift of certainty

Dreams

A talking hare
With a dead rat
Stuck on its head
What are dreams made of?
Synaptic images
Connecting randomly
From the storehouse
Of memory
The unrestrained play
Of the daughters of Mnemosyne
Digging through their grandmother's
Carved ancient wooden chest

Alchemy of Gods

"The breeze caressed your hair
Blowing gently its breath
A rose petal just fell off your breast
The wing of a bird
Covered your legs
For staring eyes
Taught you shame
The amber earthy body
Impregnated with tears
Gave birth to this aroma,"
Said an unknown god
To an unknown goddess

Rêverie on Pygmalion and Galatea

Pygmalion fell in love with Galatea
The story was told so long ago
Perhaps it was the other way around
He dreamed of perfecting her
Liberating her from the massive clay
Surrounding her beautiful body
He fashioned her diligently
Named her according to his fantasy
Her value lay
In the creature she could become
The prospect was thrilling
Visions of burning embraces elating
While Galatea in vain
Attempted to reach
His heart and mind
Welcoming ideas new and old
He was flawless
He believed
Through the hard shell
Encasing his soul
He knew it all
And did not need to be told
The arts and subtleties of love
She held a mirror
For him to see
His shadow
Lurking behind stealthily
Enraged, Pygmalion
Seized the mirror
And switched it
For Galatea to gaze
At her own misery

The Daemon's Bride

A lost soul in the wilderness cried:
"Prometheus runs in my veins
Tagore is my father
Goethe is my brother
Rivers, mountains and woods are my sisters
My pen is my lover."
"Why do you seek me then among mortals?"
A loving voice replied.
"You know they'll leave you empty, sore
And dissatisfied
A Faustian pact you made with me
The day you were born
For your soul belongs to me
I let you play and explore
Coiled around your spine I stay
And wait
Wait for you to ask
For me to give
The elixir of Gods
You belong to me my love
In the lust of my eyes
You could never be lost
In the rapture of my fire
You could never be cold
Come to me my bride
In your red crimson gown
Shake off the dull dusty brown
   Of mortal love
     And
    Come with me
Your wounded liver bleeds
But no mortal sees nor hears
For only the gods can heal
Mortals churn the poison of doom
Tears soon smear their smiles
Tragic-comedies of Gods
Mortals are actors for Gods' play
Rejoice and have fun my bride."

The Hand of God

Caught in a triangle
The wing of an angel
Stripped of its feathers
The human cobweb
Not a simple matter
It has confused
Wise women and men
The river flows
Why suffer?
All answers
Point to the way

A Scene from an Artist's Life

Red stains on snow
The shadow of a swallow
Hovers near the frozen pond
Below
Feathers quivering to the last beat of life
Above
The artist dipping his brush
Into the watercolors of life

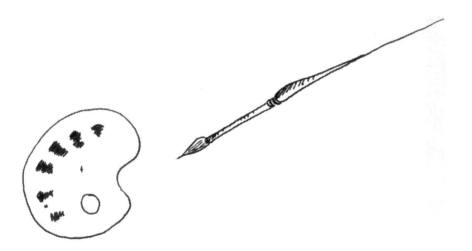

The Artist's Nightmare

Degas' ballerina
Wore a hat
To cover a hole
In her head
Shiva's arms and legs
Stamped at night
On temple walls
Covered with moss
The blue breast
Of a virgin
Fed a hungry boy
Dali colored in red
Dew droplets
Dripping down green breasts
Matisse shrouded his woman
In black shawl
And buried her in a guarded vault
A broken hand
Played on strings
Wrapped around
An odalisque's hips
A hog was hung
For Spanish plump flies
The Inquisition
Made some Satans and some Saints
In the name of a man
Who suffered and died
The artist's brush wandered aimlessly
Inside an empty frame
Searching for an essence to paint
The Inquisition is alive
Christ is alive
The ship sails
The music plays
And the birds fly

Galatea's Plea

Don't play God
With me, Pygmalion
Can't you see?
You risk to commit
What the Greeks call hubris
What makes you think
You are greater than the Creator?
Can you improve
On the beauty of trees and flowers
Or the majesty of mountains and seas?

Echo

Fleeting, I flee into the woods
Among the trees, I sing and dance
The leaves caressing my shoulders
I skip and leap across the streams
And disappear into the cave
As my grave
I choose to be
Slowly I vanish
Slowly I wither
Until I am nothing
But a whisper
Calling the last syllable of his name
A hissing
Cutting off
The last breath
I exhale.
What remains is an echo
Echo of love
Is my name

Sunset

Two crows passed
Above my head
The oyster cringed
In its shell
Playground screams of joys
Taper into silence
The afternoon breeze
Cools the weary rays of gold
Greeting of present and past

Remedy for Writers

There is no such thing
As a useless book

If you don't like it
    If you're bored with it
        If it doesn't stir your imagination
            If it doesn't speak to your heart
You can always
    Tear the pages
        Cut out the words
            Mix and match
                And make a word potion
For writers who suffer
    From depression
        Frustration
            And lack of inspiration

Mama Bear

Mama Bear
Had four cubs
She fed them well
You can tell
With every meal
She served
Morning, noon, and night
A large bowl of steamed self-righteous rice
A shot of ego booster
A guilt pudding cup
Her fence she guarded
With a thunderous growl
And threatening claws
Thick and sharp
All outsiders were shunned
Good or bad
Never mind
The cubs grew bodies
Mighty and strong
To twenty-four
They multiplied
But, alas!
To a size of a pea
Their hearts had shrunk

Mister Bird Killjoy

Mister Killjoy grew a beard
His countenance by everyone was feared
Happiness
A goal in life
He set
For his wife, children, and pet
He flew daily
To faraway lands
Toiled hard to provide
Gold, luxuries
Automobiles to ride
But all the jewels of Christendom
Caviar, sweet cakes of royal courts
Could not rejoice their wretched souls
Of luscious leaves their wishes were made
Soaring in skies above
Fragrant gardens and wise old trees
In sunshine and rainy days
Of such fickle fantasies
Mister Killjoy was distraught
And soon deployed his long time skills
To smother their hope
Dismember their dreams
Clip their supple wings
Bitter remarks he offered one
Dry pungent advice if you were around
A large portion of tactless speech
A slice of peppery criticism
Topped with hopeless pessimism
His misery he blamed you for
Marked you with guilt to the core
You are warned

Mundus Parasitorum

Parasites swarm in churches
Pious worshippers they proclaim to be
But lack civility
Basic humanity
A civilizing effect
Religion has
On their heart and soul
Assuming is guarantee
To help someone in need
Care for an ailing person
Appreciate a gift
Or acknowledge a kind gesture
These actions are all very good
When received but not returned
Hypocrites and Parasites
Are cousins in Hell
Their stench
You can surely smell

Regina Veneficarum

The queen of witches is always right
When anger explodes
Snakes and toads
Come out of her mouth
Victims will certainly avouch
But powerless heirs strongly deny
She rules with an iron fist
Judges always with a twist
To make you guilty
By her self-righteous laws
Her punishment is harsh
Unfair
Her cauldron is always hot
Prepare
When her wide square jaw
Drops down
You get caught
Between bristled bars
And mounds of sprouting warts

The Vampire Hosts

The sweet chestnut is dying
Her leaves have withered
Her fruits have shrunk
She weeps and weakens
Day after day
A swamp nearby
Poisons her roots
Galls multiply along her stem
They feed on her sap
Gnaw at her bark
Consume her body and soul
She will die soon
But her hosts will move
On and forever

Déjà-vu at Hancock Park

The heat seeps through my pores
Steaming images
Parade in grey
An ice age creature
Jumps out of a lake
Dismantled bones
Greased with precious oil
The air is thick
With heavy smoke
The blazing horizon
With threatening tongues
Encircles the playground
Of ancient dwellers
Mammoths,
Dire wolves
And mountain lions
My heart pounds in my chest
As the raging heartbeats
Of the earth increase
In volume and speed
Stravinsky's Rite of Spring
Brings back
The dead and extinct

A Japanese Scene

The earth shook

The black aged pine tea bowl

Tumbled down

A crack formed across

Its crane design

The plum blossoms

Scattered around

The tiger gone

A kimono

Thrown over

The slain dragon

Bishamonten

Lost his spear

Behind the folding screen

A young man played koto

And an old woman cried

Seven Netsuke

The old peasant
Carried a bamboo basket
On his back
Out came Otakafu
Jubilant
A girl in blue kimono
Nearby
Held in her hand
A chipped cup of tea
The Dutchman's monkey
Climbed a tall tree
The cat chased the ball
Let it roll
To the fisherman's boat
Quickly jumped and caught
The herring at the end
Of the fishing pole
The scholar wrote
What he just saw
On his unfolded scroll

A Certain Friendship

It all begins
With an ego stroke
A nickname
You feel flattered by
Lulled
By friendly hospitality
Soon you discover yourself
Charting foreign grounds
Next you realize
Your rudder
Is in the hands of others
Navigating you day and night
Suddenly you are trapped
In quick sand
You sink
No longer master
Of your own mind
You eat, drink, hear, and read
What you are told
Time and money
Where and when
Suggested to spend
If you are alert enough
Your discerning insight
Will certainly save your soul and life

Final Abode

Rambling roses
Cover the tombstones
Of the rich and famous
The Italian cypress
Rises high
Toward the sky
The lily and amaryllis
Adorn the bronze urns
The ivy thrives
In the heart
Of the Celtic cross
The narcissus and iris
Beckon the eyes
And the myrtle grows
On the graves
Of young brides
Faraway
Dilapidated fields
Of carved cross stones
Stretch in a manmade wilderness
A hallowed land in ruins
Where the wind laments
The forgotten innocents
Caravans of children burned alive
Young women shamed
Blood libation poured in the river
White bones shining in the desert
A divided psyche
Looking for a place to call home
Roams around a world
Oblivious of its pain

Prison

"Give me back my time and space
Let me out of my prison case
Free my wings of its clip,"
Cried the Monarch butterfly
"My imagination needs to soar
Out of the crypt of your collector's grip
Your cocktail parties
Swarm with beaux-esprits
Who feed on each other's
Entrails and brains
Your polluting chatter
Persuasive speech traps
Frighten me
Your false manners and crafty nets
Make me spin nauseously
Let me live in your garden instead
Where I can grow
Happy and free
And thrive among
The verbena, aster
The milkweed and lavender
To bring joy and beauty
To your heart and psyche"